Splitting Up

A Child's Guide to a Grown U

Introduction by Sophie Dahl
Foreword by Sandra Davis, Mishcon de Reya
& Dame Benny Refson, DBE, Place2Be

Psychological perspectives by
Dr Stephen Adams-Langley,
Senior Clinical Consultant, Place2Be

Some names and identifying details have been changed to protect the privacy of individuals.

All proceeds from this book will go to Place2Be.
Registered charity numbers: 1040756 (England and Wales) SC038649 (Scotland)

Anyone who was once a child will most likely remember a time when grown ups argued, and went to talk in another room, slamming the door, or saying in whispered fury, "Shush, not in front of the children!" Perhaps you heard fragments of angry words or tears through a wall, voices rising and falling, and then later, life as you knew it changed.

If that's familiar, you might be able to conjure the feeling that took place in the pit of your - very aware - child stomach, the feeling that something catastrophic and nameless was happening, made more frightening by the fact that you were shut on the outside of it, trying to catch it but also not catch it, through a floor board, in the car, dismissing it maybe as a horrible dream that would be better in the morning. Maybe you joked about it with same age siblings, or comforted younger ones, and it became part of family lexicon. Maybe you were an only child and sat solitary in half knowledge of the strange ways of grown ups. Maybe you had a family of communicators.

People fall in and out of love; this we know. Life is muddled and often muddy.

The children in this book give a voice and name to something that is frightening but common, family breakdown and divorce.

I was struck by the power of the collective young voices in this book, and feel so glad that there are support networks out there, like the very wonderful charity Place2Be, providing a forum where children do get heard and have their feelings acknowledged and held. It's crucial when you are in pain to feel like someone is listening. It's crucial that we don't raise children who are inadvertently taught that their feelings don't matter, or that silence and fear are the norm. There's a great Buddhist teacher named Pema Chodron who says this:

"If someone comes along and shoots an arrow into your heart, it's fruitless to stand there and yell at the person. It would be much better to turn your attention to the fact that there's an arrow in your heart…"

By acknowledging the arrows in our hearts, we can take them out.

Sophie Dahl
Writer and long time Place2Be supporter

Foreword

Often, the voices of children affected by family breakdown are not heard soon enough, if at all. Parents concede that their children are the most important and treasured output of their relationships, but when those relationships end children can be the ones who suffer the most. Taking into account the welfare, wishes and feelings of children during a family dispute is an enshrined legal principle, but without the concerted effort of parents to prioritise their children over their difficulties with one another, the law can only do so much.

I have been a practising family lawyer for over 30 years and, along with my colleagues at Mishcon de Reya, have witnessed first-hand the impact on children when separating parents fail to take their voices into account. The promotion of children's rights is a cause close to my heart and over the years we have endeavoured to present therapeutic alternatives to litigating over children, which rarely enriches any of the lives of those involved and can be very damaging.

This book has been created to give children's views a wider platform. Written by children who have been brave enough to share their thoughts and experiences on parental separation, we believe that the insight provided will be valuable to parents, children, advocates and therapists alike.

Confusion, loneliness, worry and the multitude of other feelings that accompany the breakdown of a family don't have a gender, class, race or religion. It is not just our parental responsibility to our children that is vital, it is our societal responsibility to listen and seek to understand what children tell us about how we can serve their needs better in the event of family breakdown.

I have worked with a number of charities and organisations that seek to improve the fraught environment children inevitably get caught up in when their family breaks down, and to address the long term psychological and emotional fall out with a view to helping those children recover or come to terms with their experiences. This book has been created in partnership with two such organisations.

Place2Be is an exceptional charity led for 20 years by my dear friend Dame Benny Refson, DBE. The charity carries out vital work in releasing the views of children who are experiencing problems, including the separation of their parents. It gives them an outlet to voice their feelings and fears in a safe environment allowing them to address, process and ultimately accept them.

Voices in the Middle is a project of the charity, Kids in the Middle. This is another wonderful initiative putting the spotlight on children's feelings, sharing advice and content written exclusively by young people of divorce to provide reassurance for others. I would like to thank both charities and, most significantly, the scores of brave children who have provided content for this book.

Sandra Davis
Head of the Family department, Mishcon de Reya LLP

There have been times when those I love have been caught in conflict. At these times it's difficult to always consider the consequences of adult behaviour, and so I turn to the words of Kalil Gibran. They serve as a reminder to me of what I as a parent and grandparent sometimes forget:

Your children are not your children.
They are the sons and daughters of Life's longing for itself.
They come through you but not from you,
And though they are with you, yet they belong not to you.

You may give them your love but not your thoughts.
For they have their own thoughts.
You may house their bodies but not their souls,
For their souls dwell in the house of tomorrow,
which you cannot visit, not even in your dreams.
You may strive to be like them, but seek not to make them like you.
For life goes not backward nor tarries with yesterday.

You are the bows from which your children as living arrows
are sent forth.
The archer sees the mark upon the path of the infinite,
and He bends you with His might that His arrows may go swift and far.
Let your bending in the archer's hand be for gladness;
For even as He loves the arrow that flies,
so He loves also the bow that is stable.

We, as adults, must protect our children from bitterness and harm. Even when worn down by conflict, it is still our duty to ensure our children's pain is given an outlet and their voices are heard, for they are the architect of their own futures and must not be the victims of adults' past.

Dame Benny Refson, DBE
President of Place2Be

Breaking the news:
the shouting and the silence

At the age of three, I remember my parents decided to separate after trying to rekindle their love for each other and giving their relationship a second chance. It was around midnight when I heard the front door slam and the car start. And that was it. My parents had separated.

El, 17

When I was younger both my parents were around there was a huge amount of arguments between my mum and my dad. When I was in bed I would hear yelling in the sitting room and I stayed awake listening to it. They did not really get on which probably explains where I am now.

Honestly, it was actually was quite scary. There were moments when the rooms were silent and I didn't know what was going on. It kept happening, but we soon discovered that it was kind of okay because that stuff was normal.

I felt confused. Really, really confused. I kept asking myself, why is this happening?

Stephen, 11

That Silence

Was it a blessing or a curse?
That Silence.
Did it mask the cracks or make them worse?
That Silence.

Were the soundless arguments
Protective? Secretive? Catastrophic?
Were the avoided conversations
Out of love? Out of sympathy? Out of cowardice?
That Silence.

Would snide remarks have softened the surprise?
Would shouting matches have stopped the tears?
Would shattered plates have been the warning signs?

My unanswered questions.
Because of
That Silence.

Abigail, 16

I found out my parents were splitting up when my mam found a new house and we went to look at it. Nobody talked to me. It just happened and I went to live with my mam. We didn't talk about it.

Hannah, 8

When I was younger I didn't really know what a marriage was, so they couldn't really tell me then, but they were still living together. I remember once they were fighting and I said stop, say sorry, say sorry... and then they stopped.

I think it was when they split houses, I realised. I thought, why are they splitting houses? My mum makes houses and I wondered, why is my mum making a house and moving into it?

I realised what was happening because my mum was organising things in her new house, and my dad was just taking the things out and giving them to her.

Adelina, 10

I was playing on my PS3 and then I saw my dad packing and I asked why he was packing. He said he was going and I asked him why. Then he said that he was leaving and that they had split up and he put his bags in his friend's car and went to my nan's house. I only found out that night that he was leaving because if I had known before then I'd have said something, but I didn't know. I was in shock and then ran to my bedroom. I was thinking, why? The next time I saw my dad he picked me up from school but I didn't ask why they broke up.

Luca, 10

My mum and dad were always fighting and she took the boys out to see the house that we are living in now. Both of them liked it so mum was like, yeah, we'll get that house. And then when mum left it was when dad was away on the Thursday or Wednesday. When dad came back we weren't there because mum left and we were all gone. I was sad because when my mum said, we're moving house, and I was like, what?

Lindsay, 8

They didn't really say they were splitting up, I could just see it coming, because they were always fighting. Then one day, when I got home from school, my dad and all of his stuff was gone. I felt like they left me all by myself. I felt like my life wouldn't be the same again, and it hasn't been, it's just been confusing and upsetting, and I just don't know what to think most times. It felt devastating, and I ended up sleeping in my mum's bed for a few months.

Anneliese, 9

A psychological perspective

Parents often believe - wrongly - that their children do not understand that they are unhappy and they wait until the children are in bed to attack or accuse each other of their failings.

However, children hear through walls and they listen to the rows and they do often despair. They are usually confused and unsettled by the ill-feeling and this can negatively affect their behaviour and academic engagement. These circumstances affect each child differently. Typically, boys tend to "act out" and become aggressive or non-compliant and disengage from lessons. Girls more often "act in" and can become withdrawn or depressed and insecure.

Small children - both boys and girls - can suddenly begin to wet the bed and have nightmares. In some cases, teenage children can begin to develop self-harming behaviours such as eating disorders or cutting themselves in a desperate attempt to divert their parents' attention to their despair and unhappiness. They are frequently fearful. I have worked with many fearful teenagers who feel withdrawn and are experiencing panic attacks due to the insecurity in the family.

Children also read the body language of their parents and are affected by the emotional atmosphere. The key message for parents is that they have to put more effort into the love they have for their children than into the animosity they may have for each other.

As Luca and Anneliese testify, the sudden disappearance of your father can be deeply traumatic. Parents should ideally work together to reassure their children and be transparent about their separation without blame. Unless their safety is compromised, it is vital that children have a relationship with both their parents. If the shouting is followed by silence, disappearance and loss of home and parent, their misery is compounded and the risk factors to their emotional wellbeing and mental health can multiply. Mediation for parents - and trying to understand the other person's point of view - is always more preferable than the polarisation of a legal battle. And ultimately it benefits the whole family unit.

Dr Stephen Adams-Langley

When a family falls apart:
pain, loneliness and worry

I did have a photo of my dad on my bedside, but she didn't feel comfortable with it after a few weeks, so she asked me if I could put it away, and I said, if it was what she wanted, then yeah.

I don't know where it is. I think maybe my mum threw it away. I wish I still had it.

Anneliese, 9

I felt weird because I never knew what was going to happen. When I started getting used to it I didn't feel weird anymore, but the way he was treating us it was like he didn't even care. I don't know how to explain it. I didn't even know how I felt. I just felt like I was by myself and that's it.
I wish they had told me and said sorry. I wish they had said they would still be there to help me. I was so mad, I got really angry and in year three I had a bad year. I was mad because I didn't have any family. I lost my family members.

Robert, 9

My parents were together since they were my age and them being together is all I knew. They stuck by each other for 23 years. I have a brother who was 18 at the time and we were all close and we still are.

My mum told me she didn't love dad anymore - that she fell out of love. As you can imagine, it's still heart-breaking no matter how old you are. Three days later she told me we were moving out: me, my brother and my mum.

All me and my brother were thinking was, this is our fault. We've caused stress and stopped them spending time with each other. My dad had depression and still does.

Sammie, 17

I didn't know if they would see each other again. I didn't know if I would see my dad anymore. I was worried that my dad might change his number so my mum couldn't get it. So I worried quite a bit.

I worry for my little sisters. Sometimes I get really worried about them. Because when they're older and they find out that our dad's gone, they might not think about him and where he might be. If I can't answer the questions they might feel alone and they might be worried all the time.

Luca, 10

I'm not bothered about my mum and dad being separated because I get on really well with my dad's girlfriend. When I'm going with my dad I feel like my mum feels that I want to be with my dad all the time and when I go with my mum I feel like my dad feels like I want to be with my mum all the time.

So when I'm with my dad I'm too busy worrying about my mum and then when I'm with my mum I'm too busy worrying about my dad. Though I've got nothing to worry about … I always think to myself, from now on I've just got to stop worrying, but it's still always there. I think about it constantly. I'll be talking about something different but I'll still be thinking, what is my mum is doing? What is my dad doing?

Bobby, 10

My dad misses us all being together and he loves all of us and always will. He just wants my mum back because he misses her so much. Sometimes, when someone talks about my mum or something, he goes on his photos and puts a picture up of her on his phone. Sometimes he goes upstairs and he cries for my mum – he goes and lies on my mum's side and he cuddles the pillows that she used to lie on. I don't like seeing him cuddling into the pillows and crying.

Lindsay, 8

A psychological perspective
In this chapter we hear of the loss children experience as a result of the separation of their parents. It is often the case that this loss translates into worry, an emotion that can be all-consuming for children who may never have experienced it before.

Robert reports that he had 'a bad year in year three' due to his internal anger and loss. This shows the potential impact on the educational attainment of children of separated parents. It is important, where possible, for the parents and the school to work together to understand the anger children may express and the negative behaviour that may occur when they act out their loss and confusion. At times like this, children can feel very isolated and vulnerable.

Parents can go some way to help minimise the confusion children may feel by providing information and reassurance. In my experience, it is always better when parents can agree and rehearse the core messages for the children. A united front is preferable, rather than the message that one parent has fallen out of love with the other, because children are not always sure what this will mean for them.

Sammie and Lindsay talk about their father's depression and the impact on them. A parent's mental health struggles, which can sometimes arise from divorce, can be a burden on the child and so it is important that parents suffering in this way seek help.

Dr Stephen Adams-Langley

Torn in two:
caught in the middle

My mum and Dad split up. I'm really sad. What should I do?

My dad wanted me to go to a Welsh school, and my mum said, no, I want him to go to an English school, because none of us in our family went to Welsh school. My mum said, you're going to an English school. And that's it. Mum and dad never talk to each other.

Joshua, 10

My mam shouted at my dad saying, you're not getting the kids back any more - they're not sleeping there. Because when it was Mother's Day, my dad got his girlfriend a mother's day card, and my mam was mad. Because if I give anything to her my mam said we won't go there anymore.

Stanley, 11

I wish my mum and my dad had stayed friends. Because now they have kind of moved away from each other, mum and dad don't really talk anymore. They face away from each other when we open the door and dad's started standing at the pathway and we hug him, he leaves, and then mum only opens the door once he's gone. And she even opens it so she can't see him. But, I think it's a bit hard for her because dad's found another person in his life.

I really care for my mum. And my dad too. I love them both. My mum doesn't really like it when I bring stuff to dad's, so I think I'm gonna have to ask my step mum to buy some new wellies for me with my pocket money.

Millie, 10

My dad has got a new girlfriend but my mum doesn't know so we are trying to keep it a secret. Once mum was saying to me, has your dad got a girlfriend? And I was like, no. Then my mum phoned my dad and went, who and where? And I didn't even say that he had a girlfriend or anything. Then dad said, what are you talking about? And then my mum was like, your girlfriend, and my dad was like, I haven't got a girlfriend.

Then when I went over that weekend the boys said, why have you told mum that dad's got a girlfriend? And then I said, I never - mum was asking if dad has a girlfriend and I was saying, no he hasn't, and then when we got home mum phoned dad.

Every weekend we go over to where my dad's girlfriend lives. My dad said, you can tell mum that we have been down there and that I've got a girlfriend, and I was like, nah I'll just tell her that we've been somewhere else.

Lindsay, 8

My dad has come to parents' evening before. One or two he's missed, and he's got angry over it, because he wants to see how I'm doing in school because he doesn't see me as often, but my mum didn't tell him when it was.

When my parents first split up my dad came knocking at the door asking if he could take me out. My mum said no because she said I was still a bit upset and he was still angry. And then he went to my next door neighbours', as they were going into their house, and told them that my mum said that he can never see me again. But my dad over exaggerates sometimes.

Anneliese, 9

I do more extra homework at my mum's house. But now she wants me to do a bit more at my dad's house, so my mum told my dad, but if he doesn't remind me I just have to do it by myself.

I watch my mum texting and the other day she wrote this thing about my homework and she wrote like two paragraphs, and then my Dad wrote two letters, o-k. They don't meet each other that much because they're not like best friends, but when my dad brings me to my mum's house, my mum just waves so he knows that I'm in the door. They don't call each other much, but they text a lot.

Adelina, 10

My parents divorced when I was three years old. Some would say that being a young child unaware of what is going on around you can help with the emotional side of a divorce, however I believe that it can be just as hard no matter what age you are when the divorce occurs.

As a child I often felt anger that I was the child amongst my friends who didn't spend time with both of their parents, as I lived with my mum and spent little time with my dad and his new wife and children.

His new relationship caused a lot of problems between my mum and him, which put me in a difficult position as a young child – I felt like I was torn in the middle as I didn't want to take one side over another.

Sophie, 16

A psychological perspective

This chapter reflects the distress children can feel when they are caught between two families, and the pressure that is sometimes placed on them "a go between". As the children explain, some parents expect them to reveal details of their ex partner's life and choice of new partner, even though asking children to communicate this information can place them in conflict.

Passive aggressive hostility is not uncommon. Nor is it uncommon for parents to threaten each other over access to the children. On these occasions, parents are often so consumed with their own emotional turmoil that they can fail to see the impact this is having. Confusion and inner conflict can be the most significant problem impacting a child's emotional health and wellbeing.

Many parents will meet a new partner sooner or later and, with that development, the issue of 'blended families' arises. This is a sensitive period for the child requiring careful negotiation between the parents and ex partners. Unless there is a risk to the child, most children benefit from contact with both their parents, which I believe must include new partners and their families and dependants. As Millie states with poignant emphasis, 'I love them both'.

Anneliese reveals that her father could not attend her school parents' evening since her mother withheld information about it. If parents are able to respect and tolerate each other, their wishes to remain involved in their child's education and life are far more likely to become a reality.

Dr Stephen Adams-Langley

New home, new family, new routine: living a double life

mam & Dad

I have two houses and im glad.

Because my mam is seferated from my dad.

when I have two home's I get spoilt alot.

my dad is getting married he's tighed a knot.

my mam is happy were she is in our home.

By the way I will never leave her alone.

I love the two os them the same.

even though I have mams sur name

when I go to my dads I somtimes Play.

I would never have it in any other way.

I live with my mum and I visit my dad. When I see my dad I cry because I really miss him so much. I want daddy to come home. I'm now allowed to speak to him on the phone and I go and stay at my dad's house. I pack a bag of spare clothes. I have clothes at my dad's but I take spare in case mam forgets to pack another set.

They have different rules. I don't get any pocket money, but my mam sometimes lets me keep the change from shopping. My mam says, do your homework straight away before you play, but my dad just says, do your homework tomorrow but do it so you don't get in trouble. I went on holiday with mam and her friend. My dad is taking my brothers on holiday but mam won't let me go with them. It's the first time I haven't gone with dad and the boys. I want mam to let me go but she won't because it's in school time.

Hannah, 8

I used to see him every week and then he got a job so then it was every fortnight. And at the moment sometimes I can't see him for a few weeks, sometimes a few months, because he's working so hard. There was one time I didn't see him for three months. I was sort of embarrassed when I came home after the second day of my holiday with him 'cause when my dad left, I got too attached to my mum and I haven't been able to stay anywhere else since. I do speak on the phone with him, but rarely because my mum says she wants to save her credit, and my dad says he wants to save his credit as well. If I had money to buy them credit I would so I could speak to him more.

Anneliese, 9

When daddy and mummy split up, I had lots of different schools. When I was with mummy, I had one school. When I finished school, my nanny came to pick me up and took me to her house and then when I was with daddy I was still in that same school for a little while. Now I go to another one.

Rebecca, 7

I feel like I'm shoved about, like when my dad was picking us up from the gym but now my dad doesn't pick us up from the gym anymore, he picks us up from the shop around the corner. Like on Monday, Tuesday and Wednesdays the boys come over to my mum's house to see my mum and they are not allowed to sleep anymore for some reason. On Friday I'd go to dad's for the weekend and I come back on Sundays.

So I asked mum if I can go to dad's for a bit and so mum phoned my dad and my dad came round and picked us up and then my mum said I can stay till whatever time I wanted. So I decided eight o'clock and then mum stopped letting us stay there until eight o'clock any other night. I don't know why, she was just not letting us.

Lindsay, 8

I don't really like to go to my dad's because he doesn't do anything with me. All I do is sit there and watch TV all day and I'm just bored. My dad's girlfriend is always mean to me. So I don't like going up there. So I say to my mum, I don't want to go up this weekend.

I want to talk to my dad in private but my dad's girlfriend is always there. I say, dad, come here, I want to talk to you in private, and he goes, no, you come here.

Fine then, I won't come. So I don't really get to speak to him in private.

Joshua, 10

My mum says to dry up in the shower and then when you get to your room and you've finished dressing and everything, put the towel back in the bathroom on a hanger or the peg or the heater there instead of leaving it in your room, because we put our school clothes on the heater in the room so they can dry more quickly.

One of my dad's rules is that when he's cooking we don't crowd him because it's uncomfortable and when we're eating we have to eat neatly on the table without moving. My mum has the same rule, but she doesn't say you can't move.

My mum has a new husband, so I have a new step dad. My dad has a daughter who is in Africa with her mum and he has a daughter in London and he's hiding it from us. It makes me feel angry because he doesn't need to lie. We already know. I have met her, but he just doesn't want to say that that's his daughter. He says it's his friend's daughter.

And then one day I asked her mum where her dad was and my dad looked and said that her dad is in Africa. I stopped asking because I got tired. She even has my eyes and her feet are like mine.

I wish he could've just spoke up and not lied and made it worse.

Robert, 9

Sometimes my parents talk on the phone and sometimes they text each other. At first they are nice to each other but by the end they are shouting and fighting. When we drop the boys off they talk but they are shouting.

One parent takes us to the other one – we get dropped off at the corner shop. Mam doesn't like dad in her street and mam is not allowed in dad's street.

Hannah, 8

I never got a choice about who I stayed with, it just so happened it was my mum. My mum became lonely and slipped into depression, and I would often hear her crying.

My dad moved away and found a new partner. When I was about six, I refused to go to his house (I still saw him, but only for a day) because I was scared of not being accepted by his new family. It took me three years to pluck up the courage to go and visit his house. Even now I do not feel entirely comfortable, and I sometimes think of my dad more as the close uncle than my dad.

El, 17

A psychological perspective

Some of the complexities of leading a double life, with different sets of rules for children who find themselves splitting their time between separated parents, are exposed in this chapter.

It is important that parents try to agree on key issues like homework, bedtimes, pocket money and access to each other. Unless resolved amicably between parents at the outset, access and visits can end up being decided by the court or mediation. This can take a considerable time to agree and resolve. In fact, it is not unusual for it to take one to three years to get these issues ironed out, which is a significant period of time in a child's life and development.

It really does benefit children if their needs and routine can be decided as quickly as possible after parents separate. It is a depressing fact, but many fathers lose contact with their children within twelve months of leaving the family home. Since many families are materially poorer following a separation, a loss or change of home and school is sometimes inevitable, leaving many children feeling insecure and confused.

Most children want to be told the truth. They are usually able to see straight through the secrets and evasion of adults, which can increase their feelings of distress and despair. Clear communication about the new circumstances backed up by consistent actions is advisable in order to enable children to form and adjust to new routines.

Dr Stephen Adams-Langley

Take it from me: advice for children of separated parents

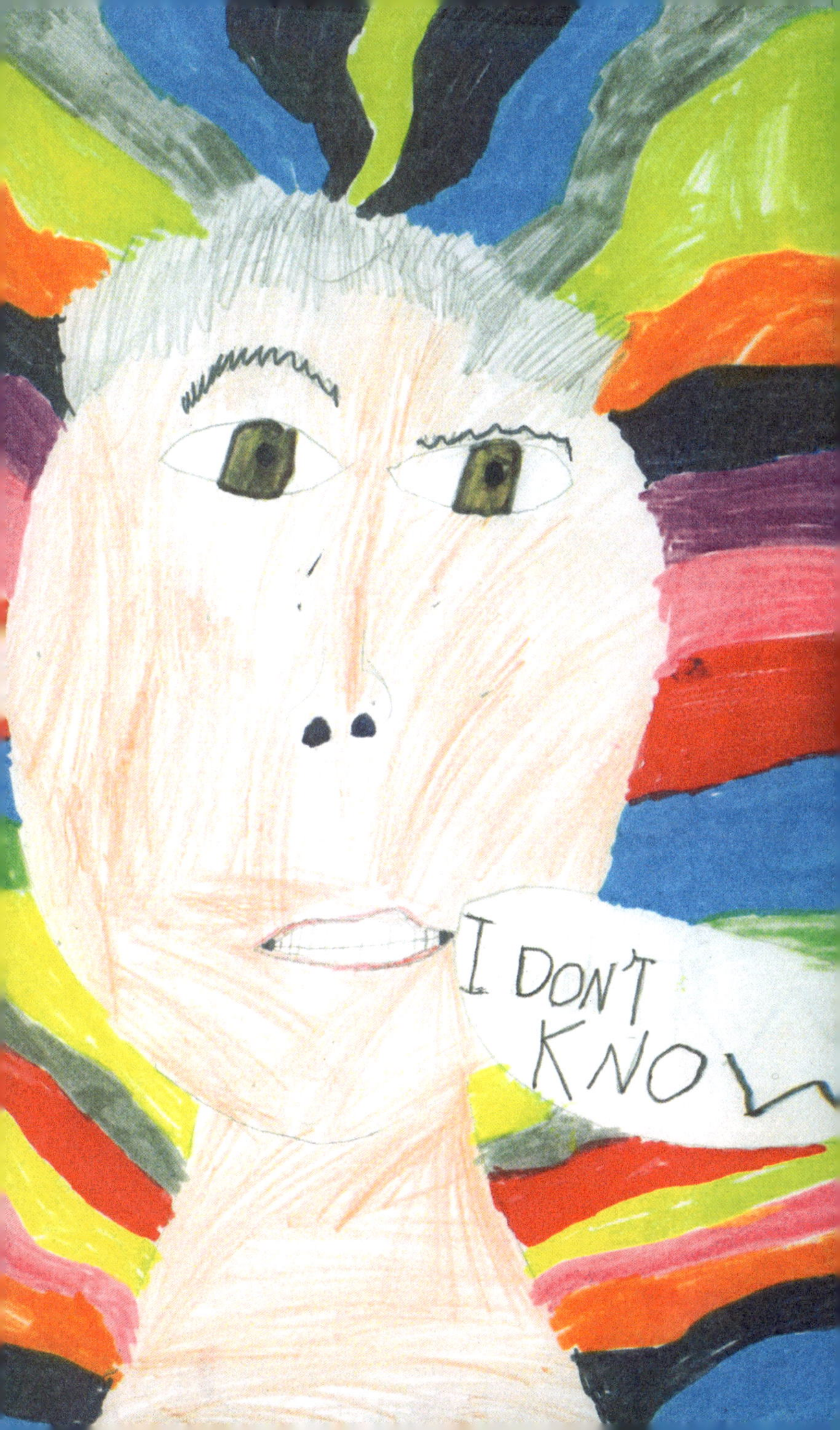
I DONT KNOW

Survival guide for your parents divorcing

1. What's happening is happening and you can't change it, so don't be too upset about it (it will make it ten times worse).

2. Get used to packing, you may be doing it every Friday, but see the bright side - it's an excuse for new clothes!

3. Your parents are going to tell you things about the other, they may be true, but don't tell the other one unless it's serious (you'll be caught in the middle of the argument) and most likely it's just one of your parents having a rant.

4. IT ISNT YOUR FAULT.
   It's very easy to believe that your parents unhappiness is because of you, it isn't (I promise).

5. It's going to be hard to adjust to new families if you get them (step parents, step brothers/sisters). You're probably going to argue with them for a while, give them a chance - you're new to them too.

6. Don't ever feel forced into anything. If you don't want to go to your father's/mother's this weekend, don't go.

7. Don't ever put yourself in a situation where you feel uncomfortable or unsafe around one of your parents. Call the other parent or, if it's serious, the police.

8. Talk to your parents. This was one of the hardest things for me, but they aren't going to know if something is bothering you if you don't tell them.

9. There's going to be a lot of crying and screaming. Your parents are going through just a hard time as you are, just be a shoulder to cry on.

10. You'll find that you will know a lot more people who are going or have been through the same as you, talk to them, never feel alone.

11. Have your own time. Don't get caught up in your parents' divorce, go have your fun and breathe. I know this is probably the last thing you could think of, but see school as an escape, don't make my mistake and let this affect your school work.

Brianna, 16

So, my mom and dad went their separate ways. For me it was heart-breaking - it was like a death in the family. I hated being around anyone apart from my girlfriend. I guess having a partner or very close best friend in this time of need is extremely helpful. It takes your mind off everything!

Personally, I attempted to ignore it. I just said that I didn't care. Deep down it was pulling me down whatever I did, and some days I would randomly break into tears and other days I'd get angry and pretend not to know why – but really I knew that it was because of the break up.

I'd be lying if I told you that I'm over it by now, I'm not. I'll be surprised if I ever am.

What I'm telling you is, don't keep it bottled up, don't let it build up into occasional outbursts, it's not good. Tell your sibling, your partner, your friend, your teacher. I'm not saying everyone must know, but seek advice in another person - it helps!

I have been struggling with behaviour at school. I'm in year 11, so this is a stressful time for me with GCSEs and college applications. There is a lot of pressure on me right now. But recently my teacher called me into her office and asked if there was a problem at home. I opened up to her and ever since the school has been more considerate towards me and really got me back on track!

So seek advice, even that teacher that you hate the most can help! After all – a problem shared is a problem halved.

Tyla, 15

You automatically think it's your fault or that you had part in it, but it's not, it's between them. People fall out of love, people have arguments. It's how things go. Just because they're not together any more it doesn't mean they love you any less. When these things happen, you need your parents and they need you. Don't take it out on yourself or others. They're still your parents and they're still going to be there.

Sammie, 17

Your parents are your parents no matter what, and they will love you no matter what. You are never to blame for their separation. I think it's better for them to be separated and happy, than together and not, because that is not a healthy environment for a child to grow up in. Ensure your voice is heard, keep your head up and remember you'll get through it.

El, 17

You look up to your parents and their relationship is something that you never expect to end. Circumstances change and it's horrible, but it isn't permanent. I promise things do get better.

It's going to be hard, of course it is. It will feel like your whole world has turned upside down, you'll be surrounded by friends who have their 'perfect' families, but sadly not everyone has that privilege.

One bit of advice I can give anyone is to sit down as a family. It's hard and really upsetting but it helps once you get through it. Stay out of the arguments (which I know I found the hardest), don't take sides and just explain how you are feeling.

Your parents will be worrying about you and how you are feeling about the whole situation more than they worry about themselves, so just open up, let them in and don't bottle it all up. You'll feel better.

Don't feel like anyone is judging you or your family because all people want to do is help. There are people and support lines you can contact, ordinary teens just like me that will be a shoulder to cry on. Stay positive, you'll get through it.

Jade, 17

My journey through dealing with my parents' divorce began when I was seven or eight. My mother told me and I was devastated. I couldn't believe that my father, the man that taught me to love and to care, could leave my mother. I cried and cried for hours – I didn't know what to say.

But as time passed, I slowly matured and learnt that life isn't all as it seems. I learnt about my parents' separation and why it happened. I'd rather see my father happy than sad. I learnt that there was no need to choose sides. I am happy that I never chose a side, because I knew my parents could teach me valuable lessons and morals in life. I found out that I needed them, that I needed both their guidance in life.

I am now 15 living with my mother, coping with this change in my life.

Isaac, 15

If I could go back in time and give myself some advice I would say, just speak to someone that you trust about it. From then on just keep calm. As time goes on you will get used to it and honestly the more you get used to it, you actually take it as a blessing instead of a curse. Because more good things happen. Your parents splitting up can be a huge thing. It can change a lot but if you stay calm you are actually going to be fine. People always say to me that they cannot believe I have no anger issues or no issues mentally.

Stephen, 11

Parents may often unknowingly make you feel pressurised to take their side when trouble occurs. A way of coping with this is to try and explain that you love them both and want to be kept out of their issues. As adults, they shouldn't bring you into arguments as this isn't good for you mentally, it can cause distress and anxiety.

Don't bottle it up if you feel like you are in this situation. Talk to your parents individually and explain how you're feeling. I now have no involvement in any discussion between my divorced parents and I feel a lot more relaxed and comfortable to contact and see either of them without feeling like I'm betraying one.

Sophie, 16

I was nine when my parents split up which destroyed me completely, I was a daddy's girl so for him to 'abandon' me hurt loads.

I finally felt as if it wasn't my fault and tried to pretend to be happy to keep the family strong, the best advice is: DON'T TAKE THE BLAME! It puts so much pressure on you.

Over the years I've become used to having one parent around, but you'll always want both parents around no matter what. I'm now 16 and I've been told that I've become so independent. I still think about missing my dad, however I have found that you can surround yourself with people you are close to and people you can trust.

Don't feel afraid to tell your parents what's on your mind because they still care about you. I've told my dad things and it made me feel happier getting it off my chest.

Don't compare your family to others, it makes it seem like your family is completely broken but in reality a new family can be made again.

Find comfort and support everywhere - teachers are the most important in school. I trust my teacher so much, she plays the role of both mum and dad when it comes to comfort.

Cerys Sophie, 16

A psychological perspective

In her 'Survival guide for your parents divorcing', Brianna urges children to accept change and to try to avoid getting caught in the middle of their parents' conflict, although this tends to be more difficult for children who are younger than Brianna. Her fourth point is key: "IT ISN'T YOUR FAULT". Many children believe that their parents' separation is somehow their fault and they often absorb a lot of guilt.

The need for the child to adapt to new family members and to talk to both parents about the emotions they are experiencing is, as Brianna identifies, very important. Her advice about not visiting the estranged parent if the child does not wish to do so, however, is less straightforward. Maintaining contact with both parents, even on occasions where the child does not want to go, is advisable in order to prevent parent-child relationships breaking down. Children usually want to please their parents and some parents can invoke subtle - and sometimes not so subtle - influence to affect the relationship between the child and the estranged parent. This can be a continuation of their anger or an expression of revenge, which can lead to the child losing contact with a parent or feeling caught in the middle.

If a child does not want to see one of their parents because they feel unsafe they should speak to the other parent or a trusted adult and explain their experience or feelings.

Brianna urges the child to be a shoulder to cry on for both parents. I feel this is a burden that no child should have to bear. Sometimes parents do lean on their children and attempt to turn them into "a best friend" or counsellor. If a parent needs to talk they should find their own adult shoulder to cry on or seek professional help through a counsellor or mediator.

Tyla emphasises the importance of not 'bottling up feelings'. This is where a school's pastoral care can really help children to process their feelings so that the child does not go off track at school. The advice from El is fantastic: 'Ensure your voice is heard, keep your head up and remember you'll get through it'.

Stephen recommends that children should speak to someone they trust about their feelings. This is where a trusted teacher, learning support assistant or school counsellor can be so helpful for children who are experiencing parental conflict and the aftermath of separation and loss. I always encourage adults, particularly those who are enduring their own emotional turmoil, to seek additional support for the child from an independent third party.

Dr Stephen Adams-Langley

The way it should be:
advice for separated parents

GREAT Tips!! (For Parents)

"Give children a reason for things so they don't get the wrong idea!"
"Keep parents close to children."
"Make sure you make the child happy!"
"Get on with the other person."
"Don't make your child uncomfortable by asking them about another person!"

Parents, don't bad mouth the other parent to your child. We want to be able to form our own opinion on what's happened and it makes us upset to see someone we love bad mouthing someone who, although you might not love them anymore, we do.

Josie, 15

The adults should try to raise a child the best they can and if that requires not divorcing then just do not divorce. You need to work hard for your child and make sure that your child has a good life.

Stephen, 11

It would have helped if I knew what was happening. If they had told me they were splitting up instead of not telling me. Instead we just moved house. That was a shock. Mam said just start packing your stuff. In my head I was thinking, what's happening?

Hannah, 8

It would be better if my parents sometimes saw each other or if we could go out for meal or something so we could all be together and have a laugh, maybe go to the movies and watch a film and that together. So then we are spending some time with each other.

Lindsay, 8

Parents should put the child first. They should always let their children see them whenever they want and whenever they can. Because they need a mum and they need a dad. Just let the child decide and tell the child that it's not their fault that they're splitting up.

Amber, 9

If a mum and dad separate and they are angry at each other they should try and be nice to each other and be calm with each other.

Theo, 6

I think parents should at least plan things before they do it. If they are thinking of breaking up, plan when the child is going to go where, and if the child is comfortable then they should always say not to worry. They should just think on the positive side of everything.

Children should be involved in the plans. If they are uncomfortable going to a certain place at a certain time then parents should make sure they tell them that they will always be safe, and they shouldn't worry and just make sure that they are happy. Be positive.

Naomi, 10

I just wish my mum had let me see my dad more. Just try and get the dad to see his children as much as possible 'cause he has the right to see them too.

Jamie, 10

To parents: never make your child choose.

EI, 17

A psychological perspective

The children say it all. As the experts here, they have lived through their parents' separation and they have a clear view of how they would like to be treated. For me, it is most important of all for parents to put their children first and to remember that every child is entitled to access to both of their parents.

Dr Stephen Adams-Langley

Acknowledgements
Place2Be
Place2Be is the UK's leading children's mental health charity providing in-school support and expert training to improve the emotional wellbeing of pupils, families, teachers and school staff.

Our support helps improve children's attitudes to learning. It builds children's, young people's and families' resilience, providing them with brighter prospects and more hopeful futures. Find out more and support us at www.place2be.org.uk.

Voices in the Middle
Voices in the Middle is a project of the charity, Kids in the Middle, aimed at supporting young people whose parents are splitting up. The project is supervised by young people who also supply all the advice on the website to offer reassurance and support to the children of separated parents. This advice is backed up by an advisory board of professionals, such as mediators and lawyers, who offer long term support. Find out more and support us at www.voicesinthemiddle.org.uk.

Mishcon de Reya
Based in London with offices in New York, Mishcon de Reya employs more than 700 people with over 400 lawyers offering a wide range of legal services to companies and individuals. It understands that a family problem or relationship breakdown is seldom straightforward. Not only can problems be extremely draining both emotionally and financially, they also have the potential to damage careers and reputations. Beyond offering a premier service for the full range of issues clients face during separation or divorce, Mishcon de Reya is also able to meet the needs they encounter in their wider personal and business lives. The Family team put children first. It handles a large number of defended relocated children cases, and is the first firm to enter into a partnership with a therapeutic organisation, setting up a relationship with the Tavistock Centre for Couple Relationships to find a better way of resolving disputes relating to children. Find us at www.mishcon.com.

Design and art direction
October Associates

Editing
Lisa Tremble, Jessica Hart, Hayley Geffin
Mishcon de Reya LLP

Print
Push

Published by Mishcon de Reya LLP
Copyright Mishcon de Reya LLP

With special thanks to Sarah Gonshaw at Place2Be

Some names and identifying details have been changed to protect the privacy of individuals.

All proceeds from this book will go to Place2Be.
Registered charity numbers: 1040756 (England and Wales)
SC038649 (Scotland)